Miguel A. Roig-Francolí
College-Conservatory of Music
University of Cincinnati

Anthology of
Post-Tonal Music

FOR USE WITH

Understanding Post-Tonal Music

Mc
Graw
Hill

Boston   Burr Ridge, IL   Dubuque, IA   Madison, WI   New York   San Francisco   St. Louis
Bangkok   Bogotá   Caracas   Kuala Lumpur   Lisbon   London   Madrid   Mexico City
Milan   Montreal   New Delhi   Santiago   Seoul   Singapore   Sydney   Taipei   Toronto

Higher Education

Published by McGraw-Hill, an imprint of The McGraw-Hill Companies, Inc., 1221 Avenue of the Americas, New York, NY 10020. Copyright © 2008. All rights reserved. No part of this publication may be reproduced or distributed in any form or by any means, or stored in a database or retrieval system, without the prior written consent of The McGraw-Hill Companies, Inc., including, but not limited to, in any network or other electronic storage or transmission, or broadcast for distance learning.

This book is printed on acid-free paper.

9 10 11 12 QVS 19 18 17 15

ISBN: 978-0-07-332502-6
MHID: 0-07-332502-3

Editor in Chief: *Emily Barrosse*
Publisher: *Lisa Moore*
Sponsoring Editor: *Chris Freitag*
Editorial Assistant: *Marley Magaziner*
Marketing Manager: *Pam Cooper*
Developmental Editor: *Beth Baugh*
Associate Production Editor: *Alison Meier*
Design Manager: *Kim Menning*
Cover Designer: *Margarite Reynolds*
Production Supervisor: *Louis Swaim*
Composition: *10/12 Times by Noyes Composition and Graphics*

Cover: Cover: Vicente Pascual. *In Illo Tempore IV* and *In Illo Tempore XIX*. 2003. Mixed media on canvas. © 2007 Artists Rights Society, New York/VEGAP, Madrid.

Credits: The credits section for this book begins on page 213 and is considered an extension of the copyright page.

The Internet addresses listed in the text were accurate at the time of publication. The inclusion of a Web site does not indicate an endorsement by the authors or McGraw-Hill, and McGraw-Hill does not guarantee the accuracy of the information presented at these sites.

www.mhhe.com

Contents

Preface

This anthology is meant to be used in conjunction with the study of the textbook *Understanding Post-Tonal Music*. The book includes detailed analyses of a total of thirty-two pieces by twenty-five composers, ranging chronologically from Claude Debussy and Igor Stravinsky to Kaija Saariaho, Augusta Read Thomas, and Thomas Adès. All these thirty-two pieces are included in the anthology. Whenever possible, complete pieces or movements have been used. If a composition or movement is particularly long, a substantial and representative fragment has been chosen for analysis and inclusion in the anthology. The remaining nine compositions in the anthology are used for analytical assignments in the textbook. The total number of pieces in the anthology is thus forty-one, by twenty-six composers. Because of the close relationship between the book and the anthology, the latter is not meant to be an optional supplement to the book, but rather an essential and required component of the pedagogical packet.

The exact correspondence between book chapters and anthology pieces is as follows:

Chapter 1. Pitch Centricity and Composition with Motivic Cells

> Analysis 1.1. Debussy, "La cathédrale engloutie," from *Preludes*, Book I (Anthology no. 1)
>
> Analysis 1.2. Stravinsky, Introduction to Part I, from *The Rite of Spring* (Anthology no. 4)
>
> Anthology nos. 2 and 3 are used for assignments.

Chapter 2. Pitch Centricity and Symmetry

> Analysis 2.1. Bartók, "Song of the Harvest," from *Forty-four Violin Duets* (Anthology no. 5)
>
> Analysis 2.2. Bartók, "Whole-tone Scale," from *Mikrokosmos*, vol. 5 (Anthology no. 6)
>
> Anthology nos. 7 and 8 are used for assignments.

Chapter 3. Introduction to Pitch-Class-Set Theory

> No pieces from the anthology are used in this chapter.

Chapter 4. Analyzing Atonal Music

> Analysis 4.1. Webern, "Five Movements for String Quartet," op. 5, III (Anthology no. 10)
>
> Analysis 4.2. Schoenberg "Angst und Hoffen," no. 7 from *Book of the Hanging Gardens*, op. 15 (Anthology no. 11)
>
> Anthology nos. 9 and 12 are used for assignments.

Chapter 5. Drawing on (and Reinterpreting) the Past . . .

> Analysis 5.1. Stravinsky, *Agnus Dei*, from Mass (Anthology no. 13)
>
> Analysis 5.2. Hindemith, Interlude in G, from *Ludus tonalis* (Anthology no. 14)
>
> Anthology no. 15 is used for an assignment.

Chapter 6. . . . And Inventing the Future

> Ives and Musical Borrowing (includes a discussion of Anthology no. 16, Charles Ives's "The Things Our Fathers Loved," from *114 Songs*)
>
> Analysis 6.1. Ives, "The Cage" (Anthology no. 17)
>
> Analysis 6.2. Crawford, *Diaphonic Suite* no. 4, III (Anthology no. 18)

The organization of the anthology thus follows the organization of the textbook, which is designed according to a roughly chronological plan and, within that, by general topics. This modular organization following two simultaneous criteria acknowledges that twentieth-century music is best understood not only in technical terms, but also in a historical context, and that stylistic and compositional developments do not take place in a historical vacuum.

An initial general topic, pitch centricity, covers music by Debussy, early Stravinsky, and Bartók in Chapters 1 and 2. The next topic, atonal music, is covered in Chapters 3 and 4. In Chapter 3, pitch-class sets are studied formally, setting the stage for the analyses of Webern and Schoenberg atonal pieces in Chapter 4. Chapters 5 and 6 discuss two seemingly contradictory, yet highly complementary, stylistic trends: neoclassicism, as found in the music of Stravinsky and Hindemith, and ultramodernism, as found in Ives and Crawford. Chapters 7 and 8 are devoted to the study of "classical" twelve-tone music, with reference to works by Dallapiccola, Schoenberg, Berg, and Webern, and Chapter 9 deals with serial practices after World War II, as illustrated by Stravinsky, Boulez, and Babbitt.

Chapter 9 thus provides a link between music before and after World War II. Post–World War II music is covered in the last six chapters (9 through 14). The general topics in these chapters, and following serialism, are issues of temporality (Chapter 10, including analyses of music by Messiaen, Carter, and Stockhausen), aleatory composition, sound mass, and other post-serial techniques (Chapter 11, with reference to Cage, Lutosławski, and Ligeti), quotation and collage (Chapter 12, with focus on Rochberg and Berio), minimalism (Chapter 13, which includes analyses of music by Reich, Andriessen, and Pärt), and finally a review of some of the most recent compositional trends as found in pieces by Thomas, Adès, and Saariaho (Chapter 14).

Miguel A. Roig-Francolí
College-Conservatory of Music
University of Cincinnati

1. Claude Debussy (1862-1918)
"La cathédrale engloutie," no. 10 from *Preludes*, Book I (1910)

Dans la sonorité du début

⟨...La Cathédrale engloutie⟩

2. Claude Debussy
"Canope," no. 10 from *Preludes*, Book II (1910-13)

3. Claude Debussy
"Sarabande," from *Pour le piano* (1894-1901)

Avec une elegance grave et lente (elegantly, solemnly and slowly)

animez un peu *(gradually faster)*
très soutenu *(very sustained)*

au mouvt *(first tempo)*

4. Igor Stravinsky (1882-1971)
Introduction to Part I, from *The Rite of Spring* (1913)

13

15

17

19

21

5. Béla Bartók (1881-1945)
"Song of the Harvest," no. 33 from *Forty-four Violin Duets* (1931)

6. Béla Bartók

"Whole-tone Scale," no. 136 from *Mikrokosmos*, vol. 5 (1932-39)

7. Béla Bartók

"Diminished Fifth," no. 101 from *Mikrokosmos*, vol. 4 (1932-39)

8.   Béla Bartók

"From the Island of Bali," no. 109 from *Mikrokosmos*, vol. 4 (1932-39)

9. Anton Webern (1883-1945)
Five Movements for String Quartet, op. 5, II (1909)

10. Anton Webern
Five Movements for String Quartet, op. 5, III (1909)

11. Arnold Schoenberg (1874-1951)
"Angst und Hoffen," no. 7 from *Book of the Hanging Gardens*, op. 15 (1909)

daß mein La - ger Trä - - - - nen schwem - men, daß ich je - de

Sehr langsam

Freu - de von mir weh - - re, daß ich kei - nes Freundes

Trost be - geh - re.

Translation of Text

"Anguish and Hope," by Stefan George

Anguish and hope in turn seize me.
My words trail off in sighing.
Such tempestuous longing assails me
That I do not turn to rest or sleep
That tears flood my couch,
That I ward off every pleasure,
That I seek no friend's consolation.

12. Alban Berg (1885-1935)

"Schlafend trägt man mich," no. 2 from *Four Songs*, op. 2 (1908-1909)

Translation of Text

"In Sleep I am Borne," by Alfred Mombert

In sleep I am borne unto my homeland.
From afar I come, over peaks, over abysses
Over a darkened sea unto my homeland.

13. Igor Stravinsky (1882-1971)
Agnus Dei, from Mass (1944-48)

Translation of Text

Lamb of God,
Who takes away the sins of the world,
Have mercy upon us.

Lamb of God,
Who takes away the sins of the world,
Have mercy upon us.

Lamb of God,
Who takes away the sins of the world,
Give us peace.

14. Paul Hindemith (1895-1963)
Interlude in G, from *Ludus tonalis* (1942)

15. Paul Hindemith
"Vom Tode Mariä I," from *Das Marienleben* (1923)

und hob ihr Antlitz auf___ zu dem und dem.... (O Urſprung na-men-lo-ſer Trä -

- - - - - - nen-bä-che.)

Wie zuerſt

Sie a-ber leg-te ſich in ih-re Schwä- -che und zog die

Him- -mel an Je ru- -ſa-lem ſo nah her-an, daß ih-re

See - - - le nur, aus-tre-tend, sich ein we-nig strecken muß - - te, schon hob

er sie, der al - - - - - - les von ihr wuß - te,

hin - ein in ih - re gött - - - -

- li - che Na - tur.

Translation of Text

"On the Death of Mary," by Rainer Maria Rilke

The same great angel which had earlier brought her tidings of her conception, stood there, waiting until she noticed him. And he spoke, "It is now time that you appear." And she was frightened as before and, humbly acquiescing, became again as the maiden. Then he became radiant and, nearing her infinitely, vanished as into her face. And he called together the widely dispersed Disciples to the house on the slope, the house of the Last Supper. They came gravely and entered fearfully. There she lay, along the narrow bedstead, mysteriously immersed in her end and in her chosen state—entirely unharmed, as one unused, listening to the song of angels. Now when she saw them waiting behind their candles, she tore herself from the abundance of voices and, with a full heart, gave away the two robes which she owned. And she raised up her countenance to this one and that one. . . (O source of nameless streams of tears.) Then she sank back in weakness and drew the heavens so near to Jerusalem that her soul, setting forth, had only to stretch itself a little, for He who knew everything about her was even then raising her to her godly nature.

16. Charles Ives (1874-1954)
"The Things Our Fathers Loved," from *114 Songs* (ca. 1917)

17. Charles Ives
"The Cage," from *114 Songs* (1906)

NOTE:- All notes not marked with sharp or flat are natural.

18. Ruth Crawford Seeger (1901-1953)
Diaphonic Suite no. 4, III (1930)

19. Luigi Dallapiccola (1904-1975)

"Contrapunctus secundus," no. 5 from *Quaderno musicale di Annalibera* (1952-53)

20. Luigi Dallapiccola
"Quartina," no. 11 from *Quaderno musicale di Annalibera* (1952-53)

1 min. 20 secondi

21. Anton Webern (1883-1945)
"Wie bin ich froh," no. 1 from *Drei Lieder*, op. 25 (1935)

22. Anton Webern
Piano Variations, op. 27, II (1935-36)

23. Arnold Schoenberg (1874-1951)
Klavierstück, op. 33a (1929)

24. Igor Stravinsky (1882-1971)
"Lacrimosa," from *Requiem Canticles* (1966)

N.B.: All instruments in this score are notated in C.

68

Translation of Text

On that day full of tears,
When from the ashes arises
Guilty man to be judged,
Spare him, O God.
Merciful Jesus, Lord,
Grant them eternal rest.
Amen.

25. Pierre Boulez (b. 1925)
Structures Ia, mm. 1-39 (1952)

26. Milton Babbitt (b. 1916)

Composition for Twelve Instruments, mm. 1-26 (1948)

27. Olivier Messiaen (1908-1992)

Turangalîla Symphony, Introduction, reh. 12-22 (1946-48)

85

86

89

90

91

94

95

96

97

28. Elliott Carter (b. 1908)
String Quartet no. 2, I, mm. 35–134 (1959)

104

105

29. Karlheinz Stockhausen (b. 1928)

Stimmung (three pages: *Formschema*, one sample page of *Modelle*, and one sample page of *Magische Namen*) (1968)

Magische Namen

RHEA Griech.: Mutter von Zeus	**AEOLUS** Griech.: Gott der Winde	**URANOS** Griech.: Gott des Himmels
GAIA Griech.: Erdgöttin	**CHRONOS** Griech.: Gott der Zeit	**DIONYSOS** Griech.: Gott der Fruchtbarkeit, besonders des Weinbaus
	DIANA Röm.: Jagdgöttin	
HERA Griech.: Beschützerin der Frauen und der Ehe	**VENUS** Röm.: Göttin der Liebe	**POSEIDON** Griech.: Gott des Meeres
	ZEUS Griech.: König der Götter	

30. John Cage (1912-1992)
Winter Music (one page) (1957)

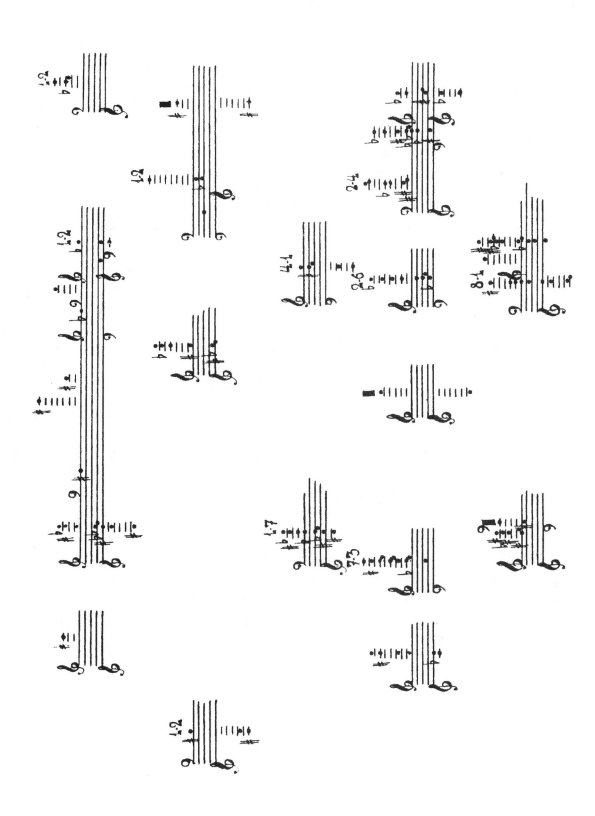

31. Witold Lutosławski (1913-1994)
Jeux vénitiens, I (1960-61)

N.B.: All instruments in this score are notated in C.

ought not to be played from the beginning but from any other phrase between two caesuras. Each musician should play his part with the same freedom as if he were playing it alone; the rhythmic values serve only as a guide and the basic tempo is between ♪ = 140 and ♪ = 150.

Sections B D F H:
The bar lines, rhythmical values, and metre are intended merely for orientation; the music should be played with the greatest possible freedom. The number of notes at places like the third bar of section B in the first viola part depends on the strength of the player's bowing (*spiccato* or preferably *ricochet*). In section D the first violin part should be played independently of the conductor and the rest of the ensemble.

Reihenfolge der Wiedergabe: A B C D E F G H
Abschnitte A C E G:
A wird von der Holzbläser- und Schlagzeuggruppe gespielt. C von Holzbläsern, Pauken und Schlagzeug. E von Holzbläsern und Blechbläsern, Pauken und Schlagzeug. G von Holzbläsern, Blechbläsern, Pauken. Schlagzeug und Klavier. Die durchbrochenen „Taktstriche" mit Zäsurzeichen darüber verlangen Zäsuren von beliebiger Dauer. Je nach Dauer der Zäsuren wird das Klangbild dichter oder lockerer erscheinen. Spieldauer der einzelnen Abschnitte: A = 12", C = 18", E = 6," G = 24". Der Dirigent gibt die Zeichen für Beginn und Schluß eines jeden Abschnittes (der Abschlag für Abschnitt A gilt gleichzeitig als Einsatz für B, der Abschlag für C als Einsatz für D usw.). Beim Abschlag eines jeden Abschnittes sollen die Musiker ihr Spiel sofort unterbrechen. Hat ein Musiker einen entsprechenden Part bereits vor diesem Zeitpunkt beendet, wiederholt er ihn vom Beginn des betreffenden Abschnitts an. Die folgenden Abschnitte, nacheinander durch Buchstaben C E G bezeichnet, sind so zu verstehen, daß

die einzelnen Stimmen nicht von Anfang an sondern von irgendeiner anderen Phrase zwischen zwei Zäsuren gespielt werden sollen. Jeder Musiker führt seinen Part so frei aus, als ob er ihn allein spiele; die rhythmischen Werte dienen nur als Anhalt, das Grundtempo liegt zwischen ♪ = 140 und ♪ = 150

Abschnitte B D F H:
Taktstriche, rhythmische Werte und Metrum dienen lediglich als Orientierungshilfen; die Musik soll so frei wie möglich gespielt werden. Die Anzahl der Noten an ähnlichen Stellen wie im 3. Takt (B) der Viola I hängt von der Kraft des Bogenstriches ab (mit Springbogen oder besser *ricochet*). Im Abschnitt D soll die 1. Violine ihren Part unabhängig vom Dirigenten und dem übrigen Ensemble spielen.

32. György Ligeti (1923-2006)
Ramifications, mm. 1-44 (1968-69)

*) The instruments in Group I sound a quarter-tone higher than written.

**) Double bass: it is written in the usual octave transposition, with exception of the natural harmonics, which are written as they sound ("SUONI REALI"). Concerning the artificial harmonics: their touch is written in the octave transposition, their resulting tone as it sounds.

*) Die Instrumente in Gruppe I klingen einen Viertelton höher als notiert.

**) Kontrabaß: in der üblichen Oktaventransposition notiert mit Ausnahme der natürlichen Flageoletts, die wie notiert klingen ("SUONI REALI"). Was die künstlichen Flageoletts betrifft, ist die Griffschrift in der Oktav-Transposition notiert, der sich aus ihr ergebende Ton so wie er klingt.

119

125

127

131

133

*) All the tremoli in this piece: as thick as possible
   Alle Tremoli in diesem Stück: so dicht wie möglich

*) All the tremoli in this piece: as thick as possible.
**) Double bass = touch: in the usual (transposed) notation; resulting tone: suono reale.
*) Alle Tremoli in diesem Stück: so dicht wie möglich.
**) Kontrabaß: = Griff: in der üblichen (transponierten) Notierung; resultierender Ton: suono reale.

137

*) All the tremoli in this piece: as thick as possible.
Alle Tremoli in diesem Stück: so dicht wie möglich.

33. George Rochberg (1918-2005)
Music for the Magic Theater, reh. 1-17 (1965)

N.B.: All instruments in this score are notated in C.

144

149

153

155

157

34. Luciano Berio (1925-2003)
Sinfonia, III ("In ruhig fliessender Bewegung"), mm. 1-120 (to reh. F) (1968)

N.B.: All instruments in this score are notated in C.

21

160

30

*) "Tooth-tremolo"

44

60

165

115

171

35. George Crumb (b. 1923)
"Dream Images (Love-Death Music)," no. 11 from *Makrokosmos*, vol. 1 (1972-73)

173

36. Steve Reich (b. 1936)
Violin Phase (1967)

$\quad$ ♩ = ca. 144

Repeat each bar approximately number of times written. / Jeder Takt soll approximativ wiederholt werden entsprechend der angegebenen Anzahl. / Répétez chaque mesure à peu près le nombre de fois indiqué

[1] see notes for pre-recording tape / siehe Anmerkungen über die Vorbereitung des Tonbandes / voir notes sur la préparation de la bande

[2] sehr geringfügiges accelerando / très légèrement accelerando

[3] tempo 1 fortsetzen / tenir le tempo 1

176

178

179

Oct. 1967

37. Louis Andriessen (b. 1939)

De Staat, mm. 1-161 (1972-76)

N.B.: All instruments in this score are notated in C.

185

*) open strings

tēn ging - ne - tai _____   le - gein tō or - thōs le - gon - ti kai en

lai _____ kai dē en rhüth - mō hō - sau - tōs pa - ra - plē - si - ō

*) no accent on low g

38. Arvo Pärt (b. 1935)
Cantus (1977)

195

197

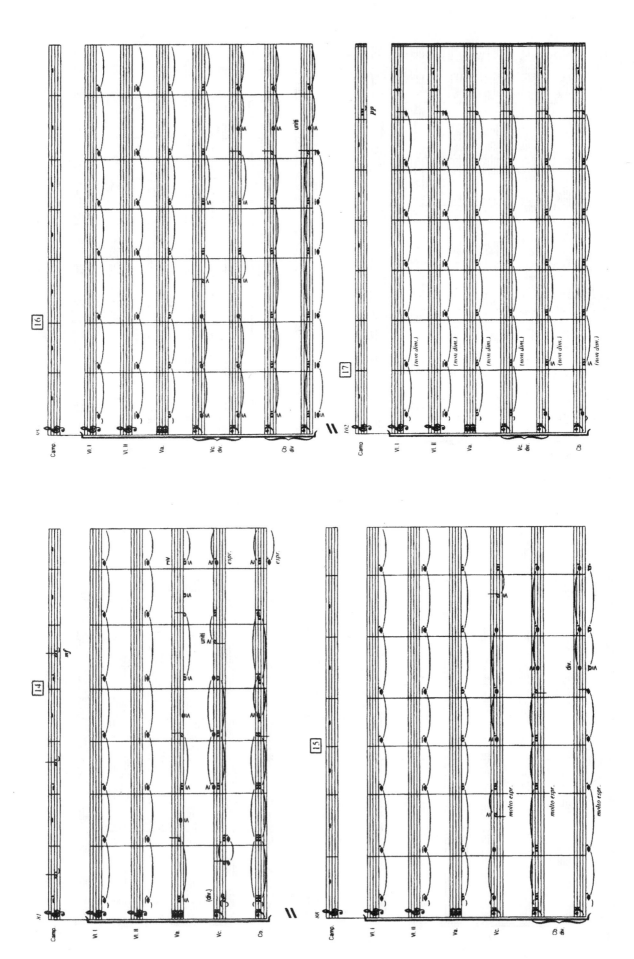

198

39. Augusta Read Thomas (b. 1964)
Spring Song, mm. 1-41 (1995)

*Play measures 16-33 as one long phrase, with subphrases of measures 16-24, 25-27, 28-30, 31, and 32.

40. Thomas Adès (b. 1971)

Asyla, II, mm. 1-43 (1997)

N.B.: All instruments in this score are notated in C.

41. Kaija Saariaho (b. 1952)
Ariel's Hail (2000)

Paris, 17 Sept. 2000

Acknowledgment of Sources